THE BIRTH OF WATERLOO

BY

JAMES R. LEWIS

3rd EDITION

REVISED & ENLARGED

BY

ANDREW FARTHING

1996
Published by Sefton Council, Leisure Services Department (Libraries),
Pavilion Buildings, 99-105 Lord Street, Southport PR8 1RH

ISBN 1-874516-03-0

Printed by Mitchell & Wright (Printers) Ltd., Southport. Tel: (01704) 535529

PREFACE

This is the third edition of James R. Lewis's 'The Birth of Waterloo in Notes and Sketches'. The title was first published in 1973 and subsequently in 1982.

Mr. Lewis spent many years uncovering 'bit-by-bit' the early history of Waterloo and this publication brought together the results of his research. This new edition has been revised, enlarged and updated. Photographs from the local history collection at Crosby Library and other illustrations replace Mr. Lewis's sketches as sadly, no trace has been found of the original drawings. As in the original text, this new publication has been arranged round historical notelets.

Mr. Lewis died in the summer of 1982 shortly after completing work on the second edition. His work will stand as a lasting reminder of his love for Waterloo and of his meticulous research into the history of the area.

Acknowledgements

Mr. D. O. Lewis for permission to revise and publish his father's original work and for the loan of his father's photographs. The County Archivist of Lancashire, Mr. B. Jackson, for permission to reproduce the map of Great Crosby Marsh.

CONTENTS

page
Introduction ... 5
The First Developments ... 7
Evolution of the Name ... 9
The Bathing Machine Controversy ... 10
Crosby Seabank in 1825 ... 13
Freeholders in 1831 ... 16
Edward Eyes' Littoral Surveys of the Duchy of Lancaster 1828 and 1839 ... 17
Ennis Cottage and the Ship Victory Inn ... 21
Early Churches ... 23
The Old Dairy and the Volunteer Canteen ... 24
The Census Returns of 1841 and 1851 ... 25
The Mushroom Growth of Waterloo ... 34
Local Government in Waterloo ... 41
The Five Lamps ... 42
The Naming of the Roads ... 43
Notable Buildings in the Area ... 46
Conclusion ... 50
Appendix 1: Population ... 53
Appendix 2: Extract from "Spas of England" by A .B.Granville 1841 ... 54
Appendix 3: Extract from "Romantic Tales of Old Lancashire" by J. Pearce 1931 ... 55
Glossary ... 57
Bibliography ... 58
Index ... 59-60

ILLUSTRATIONS

1. *The Royal Waterloo Hotel* ... 10
2. *Shore scene, with bathing machine* ... 11
3. *Waterloo shore* ... 12
4. *North Marine Terrace (Mersey View)* ... 14
5. *Marine Crescent and Green* ... 15
6. *Ennis Cottage* ... 21
7. *The Ship Victory Inn* ... 22
8. *Christ Church being demolished in 1899* ... 23
9. *The Volunteer Canteen* ... 25
10. *Map: Ordnance Survey 1845/49: Waterloo* ... 27
11. *Picton Cottage* ... 29
12. *Map: Enclosure Award 1816* ... 30-31
13. *Sandheys* ... 32
14. *Waterloo Lodge* ... 34
15. *St. John's Church* ... 35
16. *Primitive Methodist Chapel* ... 36
17. *George Rollo* ... 38
18. *Christ Church National School* ... 39
19. *St. Thomas's (St. Edmund's) R.C. School* ... 40
20. *Waterloo Town Hall* ... 41
21. *The Old Five Lamps* ... 42
22. *Mount Pleasant* ... 43
23. *Adelaide Terrace* ... 46
24. *Crosby Road North showing the Smithy* ... 47
25. *Potter's Barn* ... 48
26. *Winchester House* ... 50
27. *Carnival scene, South Road* ... 51
28. *Map: W. A. Richardson: Waterloo Local Board of Health District 1857* ... 61

INTRODUCTION

Until the start of the 19th century, Waterloo was a collection of fishermen's cottages and farms. Its development from a totally rural and isolated community into the area we know today was a gradual one. In a way Waterloo was a victim of its own natural beauty. Even before 1812, when Crosby Marsh was enclosed, the area had gained a reputation for golden sands, clear waters and wide open spaces. It wasn't until the railway was built that significant increases in the population took place and its rural identity was stripped away. These changes created a new Waterloo which was eventually allowed local self government in 1894 when the Urban District Council of Waterloo-with-Seaforth was created.

Waterloo lost its independence in 1937 when, with its partner Seaforth, it joined Great Crosby Urban District to form the Borough of Crosby. Its identity was further submerged in 1974 when the borough became part of the larger Metropolitan District (now Borough) of Sefton. Yet even with this absorption into larger authorities, Waterloo has always retained its own identity. Strangers may lump Waterloo under the banner of Crosby but to local people, they are two very different communities.

Since the original publication of 'The Birth of Waterloo', the area has undergone a dramatic re-development, particularly the demolition of Little Scandinavia in the late 1970's. While some of Lewis's landmarks have now disappeared under the bull-dozer's wheels, much is now protected, and there is wider public awareness of the importance of our architectural heritage.

THE FIRST DEVELOPMENTS

At the start of the 19th century, the place now known as Waterloo had a very isolated existence as a small collection of farms and fishermen's cottages behind Crosby Seabank (located near what is now Marine Terrace). The development of a more substantial residential area can be dated from the Enclosure of the Commons, a procedure which did so much to revolutionise the rural way of life in many parts of the country. The effect of enclosure on Waterloo was to be dramatic. The map (pp30-31) shows the distribution of enclosures in Waterloo.

In his researches, Mr. Lewis found that title deeds, which many people possess, provided essential clues when reconstructing the jigsaw of the past. His own title deeds yielded significant information about the beginnings of Waterloo. The deeds to Mr. Lewis' own house said:-

52nd George III, 1812

By an Act of Parliament made and passed in the year aforesaid instituted "An act for the enclosing of Gt. Crosby Marsh in the Manor of Gt. Crosby and Parish of Sefton in the County of Lancaster.-"

RECITING that there was within the Manor of Gt. Crosby in the Parish of Sefton in the County of Lancaster a certain open tract or parcel of commonable Pasture Land and Land covered with Sand-hills called Gt. Crosby Marsh, containing 1076^{a} 1^{r} 39^{p} or thereabouts Statute Measure bounded on the Northern, Southern and Eastern sides thereof by certain Fields or parcels of land in the several Townships of Little Crosby, Great Crosby and Litherland and the Western side thereof including the said Sand-hills by the Strand or Shore of the River Mersey.

AND RECITING that William Blundell Esquire was Lord of the said Manor of Great Crosby and the owner of divers Messuages Lands and Hereditaments within the same. And he was also the owner of certain Rabbit Warrens upon and adjoining the said Marsh.

AND RECITING that the Revd. Richard Ravenshaw Rothwell was the Patron and Rector of the said Parish and Parish Church of Sefton.

AND RECITING that the said William Blundell, the Revd. Nicholas Rigby Baldwin, the Revd. Richard Formby, John Myers Esquire, Robert Makin, John Abram, William Gibson, John Lurtin and Thomas Tasker Gent. and several other persons were owners and proprietors of divers Messuages, Tenements, Lands and Hereditaments within the said Manor and in respect thereof and otherwise were possessed of or entitled to certain Cow-Gaits, each Cow-Gait being the right of Common or pasturage for one Cow on the said Marsh.

AND RECITING that the said Open tract or parcel of Land called Great Crosby Marsh in its then present state was of little value, and the same if divided into specific allotments and inclosed, might be considerably improved, but that such division and inclosure could not be made and rendered effectual without the aid and authority of Parliament.

IT WAS ENACTED that the said open tract or parcel of commonable pasture land called Gt. Crosby Marsh should be let out divided and allotted as soon as conveniently might be after the passing of that Act. And that James Heyes of Knowsley in the said County of Lancaster, Gentleman, James Leigh of Lydiate in the said County, Gentleman, and Thomas Robinson of West Derby in the said County, Gentleman, and their Successors to be appointed in manner therein mentioned should be and they were thereby appointed Commissioners for setting out, dividing and allotting the said Marsh................

This transcript reveals how and why Great Crosby Marsh was enclosed and who was entitled to obtain land from it. The award of land was made by a commission of three local gentlemen consisting of James Heyes, James Leigh and James Woods of Walton on the Hill (the latter having been appointed in place of Thomas Robinson, deceased).

On 30th October 1816, this commission allotted the various plots of land to those entitled to them. As well as this, they planned the layout of various carriage roads (main roads), many of which still exist today. They directed that the plots should be fenced in by their owners within 12 months of the award:

"and they declared that the Sand-hills in the several allotments should for ever thereafter be kept up and preserved by them and their heirs as a defence against the encroachment of the sea and be subject to the several directions in the said award respecting the planting of Star and the general preservation of the said Sand-hills."

This Act of 1816 was duly put into effect and allotments were made to John Myers, John Abram and Robert Makin. As is often the case with early developers of an area, these three gentlemen left their mark in the form of place names. On early field maps there is Myers Marsh (north of where St. John's Road now stands), Abram's Marsh (north of South Road) and Makin's Marsh (south of South Road). Robert Makin also gave his name to a street, Makin's Lane, but this later became Hicks Road after Dr. John Hicks who lived at Makin's old residence Seafield House. John Myers is the only one of the three still commemorated locally – in Myers Road.

Even before the enclosure of the Marsh, the district was gaining a reputation on account of its fine sandy beach and clear water which attracted visitors for the bathing. To accommodate these visitors a grand hotel, the Crosby Seabank Hotel, was planned. In 1815 building was begun on the hotel and six cottages adjacent. It was the real beginning of, as yet unnamed, Waterloo.

EVOLUTION OF THE NAME

Prior to the battle of 18th June 1815, it is extremely doubtful that more than a handful of people in the whole country had ever heard of the little village in Belgium called Waterloo. Although the news of Wellington's great victory would have spread throughout the country by the fastest possible methods of the day, there would have been a significant time-lag before news arrived to the more isolated parts of the country. Thus it is not surprising that the grand hotel to be built in the area should have been planned as the Crosby Seabank Hotel and not as the Waterloo Hotel.

The title deeds of 22 Marine Terrace described how the name of "Waterloo" was instituted. In 1815 it was planned to build the Crosby Seabank Hotel and Cottages. Two years later in 1817 there was a proposal to purchase the land on which the hotel and cottages had already been built. Thus in 1818, the conveyance was made from Robert Makin to Joseph Dutton, William Robinson, Robert Bibby, John Barton and William Sutton, who became the proprietors of the 'Seabank Hotel and Cottages'. However, by 1816 the battle site of 'Waterloo' was already a household word; and the first anniversary of the great victory was celebrated locally by a grand dinner with quality wines at the opening of the 'Royal Waterloo Hotel' at Crosby Seabank. This is the first known use of the name locally. It was subsequently decided to hold an annual dinner to celebrate; and a notable gentleman George Irlam was elected as President, with John Gladstone (father of the future Prime Minister) of Seaforth House as Vice-President, and William Sutton as Secretary.

1. The Royal Waterloo Hotel showing, on the left, the original Cottages (HL14)

In 1824, there was a coach that ran from the hotel to Liverpool at 9am and returning at 6pm, providing convenient access to the metropolis. The Royal Waterloo Hotel retained its name until c1875 when it was truncated to the 'Royal Hotel'. The cottages continued to be associated with the hotel and proprietors for a few decades after their construction.

No doubt the name Waterloo was incorporated into the hotel's title on the wave of patriotic fervour that followed the climactic battle. However the name stuck and eventually came to be used for the growing collection of buildings near the hotel. Thus Waterloo was born.

THE BATHING MACHINE CONTROVERSY

The formative years of Waterloo, based on the seafront, were not without disputes and trouble; though today, many of the recorded disagreements may seem trivial and needless. One famous case is that of the bathing machine dispute of 1821. In that year the Crosby Seabank Company – proprietors of the Royal Waterloo Hotel – ran bathing machines on the shore. These grand sounding contrivances were merely wheeled wooden huts in which gentlefolk could change into their bathing costumes. The machines were pulled down to the waterfront by horses and the bathers would emerge directly into the sea. These bathing machines seem to have been an important innovation to the Crosby Seabank Company as they tried for several years to establish them against considerable opposition. No doubt the machines attracted visitors to the area and custom to the hotel.

The operation of these bathing machines was contested by William Blundell, the Lord of the Manor, who claimed exclusive rights to the strand (the shore) of the River Mersey north of Great George's Road. (The Earl of Sefton held the rights southward of this point, i.e. on the Litherland shore.) He sued not the company but an individual operator of one of these machines, William Catterall, and won his case.

A year later, Richard Westhead (a tenant of Lord Sefton), who held a farm adjacent to the Litherland shore, agreed to run a bathing machine on his land on behalf of the Royal Waterloo Hotel. William Blundell complained to Lord Sefton who, while sympathetic, claimed he could do nothing about it. Blundell then threatened to claim costs from the original court case against Catterall, but the proprietors of the hotel were defiant.

In 1823 Blundell gave permission to the Committee of owners of Marine Crescent to erect bathing machines for a nominal rent, no doubt hoping to provide competition to the hotel. In the same year, one of the proprietors of the Waterloo Hotel asked to erect further machines near old Warren House. The result of this request is unknown.

2. Shore scene, with bathing machine (SHR 67)

Five years later the dispute seems to have been resolved, as Mr. Blundell gave the new licensee of the hotel, Mr. Tower, permission to run bathing machines. After this, bathing machines seem to have become less of an issue and are rarely mentioned again except in more pleasurable terms.

Jane Welsh Carlyle (wife of the famous writer Thomas Carlyle) described the foreshore in the 1840's when she was staying with relatives in Seaforth:

"There are nice machines constructed for the use (to change in)...*the water looks clean and there is a nice sandy beach".*

A great local character of the time was Reverend Richard Rothwell who came down from Sefton Church daily in his yellow gig to bathe in the Mersey.

3. Waterloo shore, at the turn of the century (SHR 15)

In 1884 the Waterloo-with-Seaforth Local Board of Health (the local authority) leased the foreshore from Colonel Nicholas Blundell for 21 years for £1 (though the Colonel reserved the right to licence bathing machines). Ten years later this leasing arrangement became a more permanent feature. For reorganisation of local government in 1894 created a local council (for the Urban District of Waterloo-with-Seaforth) which had wider powers than the old Local Board. Queen Victoria as Duke of Lancaster, granted the new authority the foreshore lying within its boundaries for the price of £25. Thus, the foreshore area passed out of private control and into the public domain.

Bathing machines were still used even after Queen Victoria's reign was over and their proper use *"for preventing any indecent exposure of the persons of the Bathers"* became enshrined in the Urban District's bye-laws. The posts marking the standing places for bathing vans were finally removed from the Waterloo shore in 1911.

CROSBY SEABANK IN 1825

Within the first ten years of the construction of the hotel, the population of Crosby was recorded in the 'Directory and gazetteer of the County Palatine of Lancaster' by Edward Baines. This directory, the earliest of its kind for the area, lists the main residents in the chapelry of Great Crosby, and indicates those living at Crosby Seabank. The information that Baines collected identifies three streets; South Street, Marine Crescent and East Street. The majority of occupations of the principal residents appear to be service-related.

South Street

William Yates — Postmaster and Grocer.
Richard Johnson —
Mrs. S. Barber — Lodginghouse Keeper
Mrs. Greenhalgh — Lodginghouse Keeper
William Wright — Farmer

Marine Crescent

John Bird — Architect
John Kilshaw — Joiner, etc.
Miss Elizabeth Peet — No. 11

East Street

Ellen Cunningham — Poulterer and Pastry Cook
James Hodgson — Liquor Merchant
Mrs. Broadbent — Lodginghouse Keeper
Mrs. H. Catterall — Agent for the letting of houses
Thomas Worthington —

Waterloo Hotel:

Mary Bates

North Marine Terrace

One of the streets mentioned in Baines' directory, but not actually marked as part of Crosby Seabank, is North Marine Terrace. Now named Mersey View, this street was in the area known as Brighton le Sands, though still part of the future Urban District of Waterloo-with-Seaforth. As it was one of the earliest streets in the locality, containing some magnificent buildings, it is worthy of mention.

4. North Marine Terrace (Mersey View) probably in the 1860s (RD/MERV 1)

Built in 1822-23 North Marine Terrace had an excellent view of the River Mersey; the name changed to Mersey View in approximately 1867. The houses now numbered 2 to 10 show very few signs of alteration and, with their stone framed Gothic upper windows and large bay windows downstairs, form an interesting architectural unit. No. 2 Mersey View has a particular niche in history. Known as 'Ivy Deane' it was home to 'The Ladies Guild' and served as a Registry of Domestic Service, at a time when a large proportion of the population in the area were domestic servants.

The houses numbered 12 to 14 have been altered and they complete the section built in 1823. According to the 'Victoria Review' of June 1936, the group of houses numbered 26 to 32 were built in 1822, though little of their original outside appearance has survived.

Marine Crescent

5. Marine Crescent, with cows grazing on the Green (RD/MARC 5)

When Baines was compiling his directory, Marine Crescent must have been brand new. The 'Annals of Liverpool' at the back of the Gore's 'Directories of Liverpool and Environs 1898', state that Marine Crescent was built in 1825, the year Baines published his work. Either Baines visited Waterloo just before building was begun on the new road or Gore's date is slightly inaccurate. It is unlikely that it was all built within one year, but it was certainly completed before the other terraces and must have been considered an address of some distinction, as may be seen in the way it has been singled out in the following list of Freeholders.

FREEHOLDERS IN 1831

A list of Great Crosby's freeholders (people who hold land or property for life, free of manorial influence) was compiled six years after the publication of Baines' directory. The freeholders of Great Crosby were entitled to vote for a Member of Parliament for the County of Lancaster. Most people in Waterloo held their land in copyhold (i.e. they were tenants subject to manorial dues) but there were some freeholders who would have been people of some influence in the area in 1831. The freeholders of Great Crosby at this time were:

Robert Mawdsley
James Mawdsley
Edward Bradshaw
William Davies
Mr. Johnson (Gent.)
John Blankhorn
Thomas Davies
Wm. Leatherbarrow
Richd. Johnson (Crescent)
James Formby (Moore Lane)
Joseph Blanchard
Thomas Westhead
Thomas Wright
William Bellion
John Howard
William Lupton
William Bennett
Thomas Heyes
Robert Heyes
William Arnold
Henry Arnold
Thos. Worthington
James Orrell
Henry Wright (Crescent)
Thos. Smith (Crosby Marsh)
Richard Lorrimer
Richard Bond
Richd. Waddington (Crescent)
Jas. Williams
Henry Green
Mr. Spencer (Thornton)
Mr. John Lupton
James Kaye
Henry Harrison (Litherland)
Mr. Brettargh
John Westhead (Crosby Mill)
John Somner
Samuel Weston
Henry Bellion
Thos. Rothwell
Francis Goodchild
John Formby
George Orme
William Holden
Thomas Taylor (Warren Gutter)
Mr. Gleadah (Marsh)
Mr. Towers (Hotel)
Mr. Makin
John Davies
Joseph Bradshaw
Timothy Bradshaw
John Bradshaw
Samuel Bradshaw
Thos. Woods (Village)
John Winstanley
Richard Brown
Mr. Hooton
William Turton

Although only some of the freeholders are given an address, this list is still useful. Names from this list keep appearing in early documents of the area and some, like the Arnolds, are recorded in the area for hundreds of years. The locations that are given indicate local names for places at the time. Warren Gutter is an interesting example as it relates to a ditch on the rabbit warren, and there is the retention of the name Crosby Marsh, fifteen years after its enclosure.

EDWARD EYES' LITTORAL SURVEYS OF THE DUCHY OF LANCASTER 1828 AND 1839

Another contemporary document was prepared by Edward Eyes, a cartographer who produced maps of Liverpool and the surrounding area. In 1828 Eyes had toured the Duchy of Lancaster and surveyed the land and people. His tour in 1839 was made for the Conservancy of the coast and listed owners of land fronting the sea. It provides very useful information. The area included locally covered the strip of coast from Rimrose Brook which was the southern boundary of the township of Litherland, to its northern boundary at Great George's Road; then on through the township of Great Crosby to the River Alt. It names the people living in the area and shows the plots on which houses had already been erected. What we now call Waterloo is covered partly by the survey of Litherland and partly by that of Great Crosby.

This extract of Eyes' 1839 survey covers Waterloo and starts at the Rimrose Brook boundary. A complete transcription can be found in the Proceedings of the Historic Society of Lancashire & Cheshire 1869/70.

A Littoral Survey Of the Port Of Liverpool:

Being a survey and account of the encroachments and embankments, with other memoranda relative to the Strand of the Mersey, commencing at Hilbre Island, situate in the entrance of the River Dee, and extending over each township in the County of Chester to Frodsham and Warrington Bridges, and thence over each township in the County of Lancaster to Formby Point. By Edward Eyes.

Township of Litherland. Parish of Sefton.

This township is situated near the entrance into the Mersey, and although much exposed to the sea, the lands abutting it do not appear to suffer so much as formerly. This may be accounted for by the change which has been gradually and imperceptibly taking place in the direction of the principal stream entering into the river, and to the constant accumulation of drift sand in some degree making up the waste occasioned by tide water. No material changes take place in the tide marks.

The Right Hon. the Earl of Sefton is Lord of the Manor, for which a court is regularly held. His Lordship claims also the exclusive right to the strand, and in several sales lately made adjoining thereto, purchases are restricted from using it except for bathing upon, passing over and taking sand, gravel &c., according to the conditions of their respective agreements.

Names of the Owners of Land fronting the sea:-
Rimrose Brook, boundary of township.
Mr. James Muspratt. House and Land.
Mr. Henry Francis Penny. House and Land.
Part of the strand enclosed.
Private Road.
Mr. Robert Bickersteth. Land.
Mr. William Potter. Land.
Open to the beach.
Private Road.
Messrs. John Bibby and William Potter. Land.
Private Road.
Mr. Thomas Avison. Land.
Mr. John Kilshaw. Land.
Enclosed in front by rails about the line of high water.
Thomas Belshaw. Land.
George Crosfield. House and Land.
Thomas Avison. House and Land.
Miss Avison. House and Land.
Enclosed in front by rails about the line of high water.
Robt. Lund Roberts. Two Houses and Land.
Rev. John Jones. House and Land.
Mr. John Kilshaw. House and Land.
Open to the beach

Township of Great Crosby. Parish of Sefton.

This township is below the entrance or mouth of the river and lies open to the sea.

The land, although much exposed is little affected, except about Crosby Point, by its waters in consequence of being in part protected by a barrier of sandhills, and the drift sand filling up the waste occasioned by the wash of the tide.

The line of high water seems to be receding, but that of low water does not materially alter.

There are not any enclosures on the strand.

William Blundell, Esq, is Lord of the Manor; claims the exclusive right to the strand; and unless under special agreement, restricts persons owning lands abutting from the use of it, except passing over.

Proprietors of lands on the edge of the sea:-

Great George Road.

Proprietors of the Crosby Sea-Bank Hotel and Cottages. Hotel and Land in front.
The same proprietors. Six cottage-houses and Land.
John Kilshaw. Land.
Thomas Smith. House and Land.
Robert Rawstorne. House and Land.
John Kilshaw. House and Land
Mrs. Myers. House and Land.
— Fisher. House and Land.

South Road.

John Broadbent. House and Land.
Margaret Bird. House and Land.
John Van Zeller. House and Land.
John Kilshaw. House and Land.
Margaret Bird. Two houses and Land.
The Rev. Fred. Anson. House and Land.
Margaret Colley. House and Land.
John Van Zeller. Three houses and Land.
William Watmough. House and Land.
John Williams. House and Land.
Thomas Mellor. House and Land
Margaret Bird. House and Land.
Richard M. Beckwith. House and Land
George Holden. House and Land.
Mrs. Jones. House and Land.
Miss Mary Rowe. Two Houses and Land.
Mrs. Ellen Gaskell. Two Houses and Land.
Miss Robinson. Two Houses and Land.
— Western. House and Land.
Joseph Holland. House and Land.
Joseph Mason. Two Houses and Land.
Major Rowe. House and Land.

Kent Street

William Lupton. Three Houses and Land.
Edward Gilling. Land.
Mary Hardly. Land.
Edward Burin. Land.
John Postlethwaite Padley. Land.
Charles Padley. Land.

Edward Gilling. Land.
Mary Hardly. Land.
Edward Burin.
Thomas Aquiline Dale and Richard Halberd. Land.
— Chaffers. Land.
The Rev. — Formby. Land.
Charles Horsfall. House and Land.
Private Road.
— Greenall. Bath and land
James Williams and Co. Land.
Rail Greenhorn and Thomas Lower. Land.
Thomas Tasker. Land.
William Blundell, Esq. Sand-hills and Warren.

Not only are land owners named but the extent of their holdings is listed and located. Several people are shown to have more than one house and plot of land in the area, perhaps indicating a higher degree of wealth or a property speculator. Further information can be deduced from the survey. In the final group of names shown in the extract listed by a Private Road is "— Greenall. Bath and Land". Lewis suggested this had a connection with the bathing machine controversy of 1823, but it may have further connotations. Perhaps Greenall's bath, the only one listed specifically, was a local 'landmark' and led to the naming of Bath Street?

Several notable people are mentioned in the survey, people who figure prominently in national as well as local history. Perhaps foremost among these is James Muspratt. He arrived in England in 1823 from Dublin and started the manufacture of alkali on a large scale at his Vauxhall Road works in Liverpool. The success of this enterprise enabled him to finance the building of Seaforth Hall in 1840. The hall stood on the site of the present Royal Seaforth Dock, but was demolished about 1924, well before the dock's construction.

On the site of the same modern dock complex was the residence of John Bibby, the shipping tycoon. Such was his family's standing that up until the building of the Royal Seaforth Dock, the Seaforth 'shore field' was known as Bibby's land. In Eyes' survey, Bibby's co-owner is William Potter. He built Potter's Barn, the first phase of a grandiose complex which was never completed. This land was the cause of dispute in 1903 when Mrs. Bibby decided to sell the land to Waterloo-with-Seaforth UDC to create a recreation ground. Before the deal was finalised, the Mersey Docks and Harbour Board stepped in and offered Mrs. Bibby a substantially inflated price for the land. She sold the land to this new bidder for £16,000 but was sued by the Council who were awarded £11,500 compensation as well as a 7-acre site on Bibby's land.

Eyes' survey listed adjacent plots of land owned by John Kilshaw and Thomas Avison. These were sold and two notable buildings were constructed on the site. Today this land is part of Waterloo Road, and the two buildings are Ennis Cottage and the old Ship Victory Inn.

ENNIS COTTAGE AND THE SHIP VICTORY INN

Ennis Cottage

Ennis Cottage is number 58A Waterloo Road. This, with No. 58 next door and the house in Brunswick Mews which was the Ship Victory Inn, completes a group of listed buildings of special architectural interest. Ennis Cottage and the adjoining residence were originally designed as two dwellings, although they do look like one Regency-style house. The Deeds to Ennis Cottage begin with the conveyance dated 10th April 1829, from Thomas Avison and John Kilshaw to Charles Ammes, of land in Litherland Marsh on the west side of a street called Waterloo Road.

6. Ennis Cottage, Waterloo Road (J. R. Lewis)

A note dated 9th April 1829 states that Charles Ammes was building two houses fronting on Waterloo Road. This is followed by a conveyance from Chas. Ammes, plasterer, and Geo. Highton, surveyor, to Miss Catherine Houghton. Sometime around the late 1830's the entire building became known as 'Southwell Cottages' (as named on the Ordnance Survey map 1845-9). In 1846 there was a conveyance from Mr. P. Tasker to the Rev. Charles John Graham Jones, incumbent of Christ Church. Evidently the two houses were then combined and became the Vicarage for Christ Church.

The Rev. C. J. G. Jones died in 1850, but the next conveyance was in 1883 from the Rev. Charles Edward Graham Jones (probably the son of the Rev C. J. G. Jones) to James Rawsthorne of one house, formerly two. A note stated *"The houses in one tenement lately occupied by Mrs. Harriet Rowson"*. Who Mrs. Rowson was or how she came to be living at the house is not known.

The Ship Victory Inn

Today, this building is a private residence, but originally it was constructed as an inn. Unfortunately, like many pieces of local history, the deeds to the building were destroyed in the Blitz. All that remains is a schedule which recorded a release, dated 8th April 1836, from T. Avison and John Kilshaw to Absolom Neal and another; though the schedule does not state whether there was a building on the site at the time. The Inn however, may have been constructed as early as 1829. This is supported by the deeds of Ennis Cottage which state that the cottage was bounded on the west by an intended back street to be made on the land of Thomas Avison and John Kilshaw, thus suggesting a building on the Inn's site.

7. The Ship Victory Inn, Brunswick Mews (HL 17)

The 1841 Census lists an entry "Absolom Neal, publican, The Mews, Waterloo", and Richardson's map of 1857 shows the building marked as "The Ship Inn". Various directories show Absolom Neal in possession until 1868, when Margaret Neal is named as publican. The last mention was in 1873 after which the building evidently ceased to be an inn.

EARLY CHURCHES

Old Christ Church

The first Christ Church was built in 1840, being extended further in 1851 and 1859. Originally it was intended to provide a place of worship for the many visitors that came to the area on holiday. In 1890 a bulge appeared in the south wall of the church and it was found that ivy had caused substantial structural damage. Although the building was pronounced safe, it was decided to rebuild the church totally. In 1899, the old church was demolished and on 2nd December of that year the current building, designed by the famous architects Paley and Austin, was consecrated.

8. Christ Church being demolished in 1899 (CH 9)

The Independent Chapel

This building was next to the Volunteer Canteen in East Street until its demolition c1976. It was a building that underwent as many transformations as the environment around. It was built by Richard Waddington in 1840 as a Methodist Chapel, and seated 300 people. In 1865 it was known as 'The Independent Chapel' but by 1868 it was being described as 'The Primitive Methodist Chapel'. Just three years later it had been transformed into St. John's Sunday School. After only another two years, it was changed again being the 'Assembly Rooms' in 1873, and later in the 1880s, the theatre for the Waterloo Amateur Dramatic Society.

During the Boer War it was used as a volunteer drill hall, but by 1906 it was in the possession of another army, the Salvation Army. In 1909 the building was adapted again to become the Bijou Theatre, providing a variety of entertainment including early cinema. In 1917 it concentrated entirely on this new entertainment as the Bijou Electric Picture House until 1922 when it closed.

Following that, it became a depot of a bus service, a taxi-cab company's office and a cycle repair shop.

THE OLD DAIRY AND THE VOLUNTEER CANTEEN

The building that was once the Independent Chapel formed a group with two other structures, one which was once a dairy, the other a private house.

John Abram of Thornton, having received a parcel of land under the Enclosure of the Commons Act 1812, conveyed one portion to John Kilshaw, joiner, and John Bird, architect, in 1820. Seven years later in 1827, Kilshaw and Bird sold the land to Roger Gaskell. This plot was bounded on the north by the house of Richard Waddington, which later became "The Canteen Vaults". Gaskell proceeded to build two coach-houses which backed on to Mason Street, together with stables, wash-house and other buildings.

In 1842, Roger Gaskell bequeathed the property to James Hallows. Two years later he in turn conveyed the property to James Hallows the younger. Included was a house which had been erected since 1842, replacing a cottage which had been demolished. By 1869, this house had been divided into two, one half becoming the dairy farm of William Rimmer. The other half of the building had several uses. Firstly it became James Emblem's beer sellers shop, by 1870 it was 'Halls the Carriers', and by 1924 it was Jane Rimmer's greengrocers.

The neighbouring private house of Richard Waddington had become, by 1871, Richard Waddington, Beerseller, and subsequently in the 1880s Richard Waddington's "Canteen Vaults". It had become "The Volunteer Canteen" by 1906, and is presumed to have been thus named because of the volunteers who used the Independent Chapel as a drill hall during the Boer War.

The date on the front of the building, 1924, refers to a face-lift it received that year.

9. The Volunteer Canteen, East Street, with on the right - the Independent Chapel (unclassified)

THE CENSUS RETURNS OF 1841 AND 1851

The census of 1841 was the first in which a record was made naming individuals instead of merely recording population figures. For the first time the complete inhabitants of an area were listed and this gives us a fuller local picture. The 1841 and 1851 censuses are also important because they come before the mushroom growth of Waterloo yet it is listed as a specific area. The information contained in each census is detailed, and basic data on Waterloo's population and streets can be identified.

Census of 1841

Under the heading of "Chapelry of Great Crosby" in "the part called Waterloo" various streets and other features are shown. These are:

Mount Pleasant, East Street, back of Crescent, Bath Buildings (now The Marine Hotel), *York Street, York Square, York Place, The York Hotel, Hotel Tap, South Road, Waterloo Hotel, Waterloo Cottages, Waterloo Terrace, York Hotel Yards, Wellington Hotel (now The Queens Hotel), Marine Crescent, Adelaide Terrace, Mews Waterloo, Brunswick Parade, Great George's Road, Brighton, Brook House, Brighton Road (now Brooke Road), Waterloo Cottage.*

The Publicans shown are:

York Hotel	—	*William Jones, Innkeeper.*
Waterloo Hotel	—	*Mary Ann Towers.*
Wellington Hotel	—	*William Ellams, Publican.*
Mews Waterloo	—	*Absolom Neal, Publican (The Ship Victory)*
East Street	—	*James Livingwood, Beerseller.*
Brighton	—	*Mary Taylor, Innkeeper*

The population given for 1841 was 699 for Waterloo (the part in Litherland Township) and 649 for Great Crosby/Waterloo (the part in Great Crosby Township). The small number of streets indicate Waterloo's lack of development. However the large number of hotels in comparison with the population is not surprising — Waterloo was a community which expanded primarily in response to the influx of visitors attracted to its unspoilt beaches.

It is interesting to compare the 1851 Census with its immediate predecessor. During the intervening years, Waterloo's development had been gradual, without the explosion in population and building that was to characterise later years.

Census of 1851

The Census returns of 1851 show some changes in the structure and names of the local streets and other features:

Marine Crescent, East Street, Mount Pleasant, Arnolds Place, York Square, York Street, York Place, Waterloo Terrace, Royal Waterloo Hotel, Waterloo Cottages, Bath Road, Bath Street, Kilshaw Terrace, Back Kilshaw Terrace, South Road, Bath Hotel, Back South Road, Brighton Road, Liverpool Road (now part of Crosby Road North), York Hotel, North View, Brighton, North Marine Terrace, Brighton Road (now Mersey View), "Brooke House", "Sandheys", Brighton Road (now Brooke Road), Victoria Cottage, Adelaide Terrace, Picton Cottage, Crosby Road. (The address of Absolom Neal, Publican, and John Jones, Incumbent and Rural Dean of Christ Church, is given simply as "Waterloo")

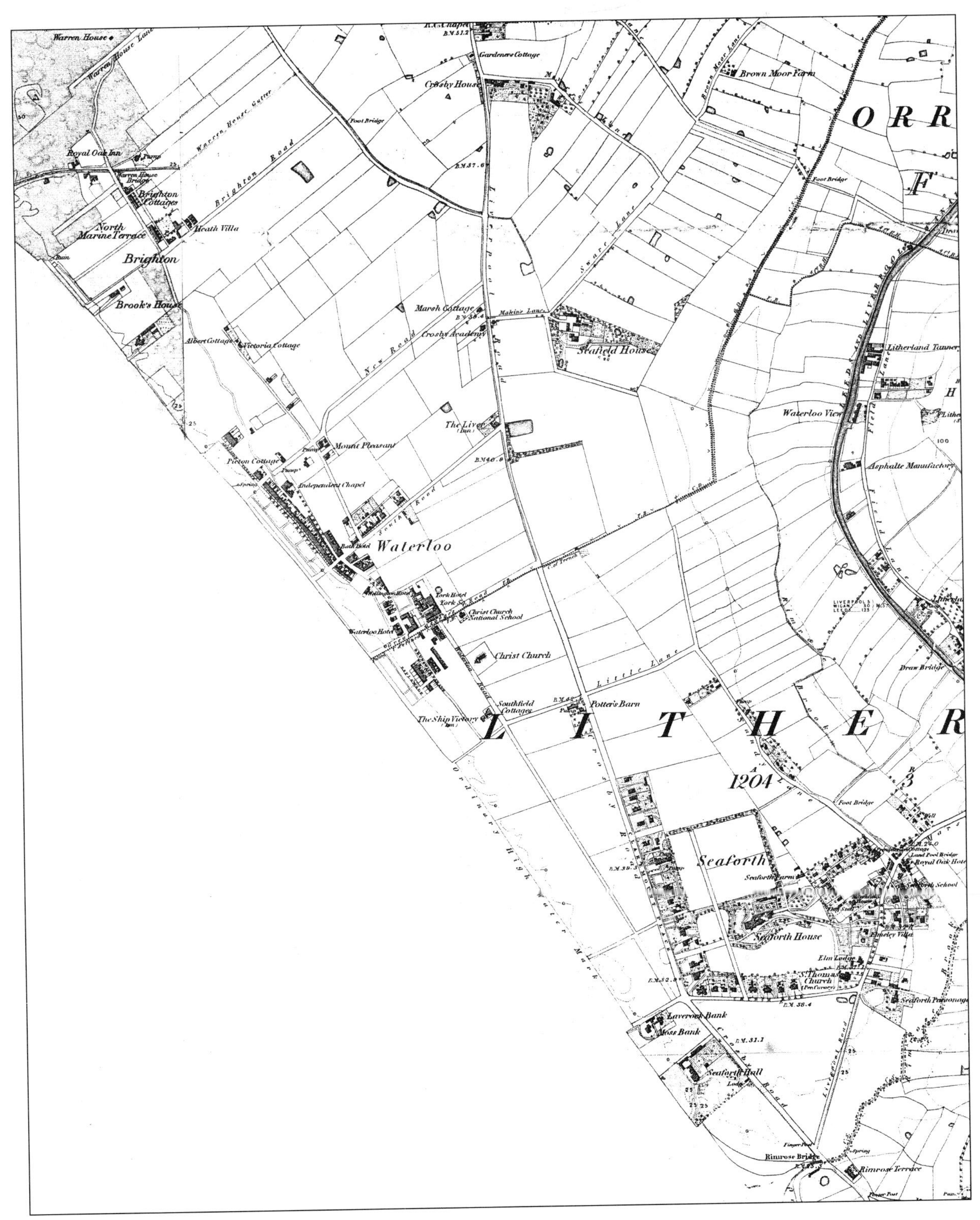

10. Map: Ordnance Survey 1845/49: Waterloo (M 406)

The Publicans shown are:

Royal Waterloo Hotel	—	*William Howarth.*
Bath Hotel	—	*John Robert Gibson and Thos. Brining (retired)*
South Road	—	*George Orme, Farmer, 5 acres and Beerhouse Keeper.*
Liverpool Road	—	*Mary Lupton, Licensed Victualler's wife.*
York Square	—	*John Harrison, Beerhouse Keeper.*
York Street	—	*Edward Sumner, Licensed Victualler*
Brighton	—	*Mary Marrow, Publican*
Waterloo	—	*Absolom Neal, Publican (The Ship Victory)*
South Road	—	*Thomas Neal Tyrer, Licensed Victualler.*

The individual houses shown are:

"Brooke House"	—	*Charles Leigh*
"Picton Cottage"	—	*John Padley*
"Sandheys"	—	*Richard Houghton (timber merchant)*
"Victoria Cottage"	—	*Lieut. Henry G. Killack, R.N.*

The population listed for Waterloo at the 1851 Census was 859 for Waterloo (part of Litherland Township) and 816 for Great Crosby/Waterloo (part of Great Crosby Township): a modest increase on 1841. It is interesting to note the differences in street names, including the arrival of Liverpool Road. Another development is the emergence of local family names being incorporated into the street-names. Arnolds Place and Kilshaw Terrace both refer to families that had been involved with Waterloo since its early beginnings.

From the 1850s onwards, Waterloo expanded substantially in population and development. This growth can be attributed to several factors: the popularity of the sea front which attracted visitors (and thus business) to the area; its close proximity to fast growing Liverpool, and most importantly the construction of a railway from Liverpool to Crosby. This final factor was probably **the** crucial event in Waterloo's development and after it was built, the population exploded.

The 1851 census is also interesting because it names several individual houses. Surprisingly, these were not necessarily the most notable buildings in the area. The buildings are:

Brooke House

Charles Horsfall, a Liverpool merchant, was shown on Edward Eyes' survey as having a house and land in the area. The 1841 census reveals its name, "Brook House". Horsfall probably chose this name because a brook flowed close to the building. The brook was forced underground in 1935 with the construction of new houses. The spelling of this house changed on documents from Brook House on the 1841 census, to Brook's House on the 1845-9 Ordnance Survey map, and finally settled as Brooke House. By the 1851 census, Horsfall's house was in the hands of Charles Leigh who retained the name given to it by the original owner. Charles Leigh, aged 59 at the time, is listed as a manufacturer of earthenware. No doubt it is this house which gave its name to Brooke Road, (originally known as Brighton Road).

Picton Cottage

11. Picton Cottage, Wellington Street (RD/WEL 3)

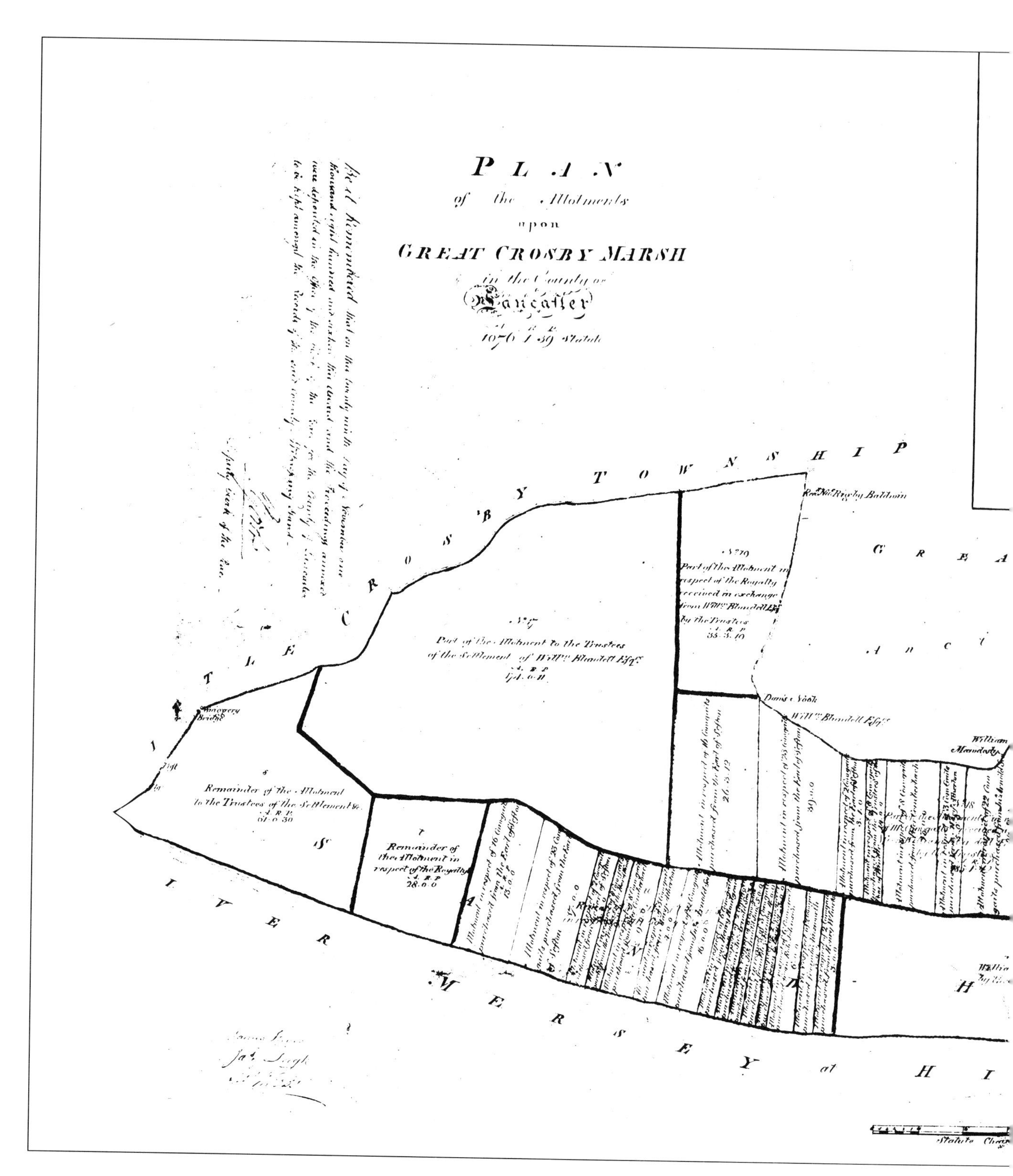

12. Map: Great Crosby Marsh: Enclos

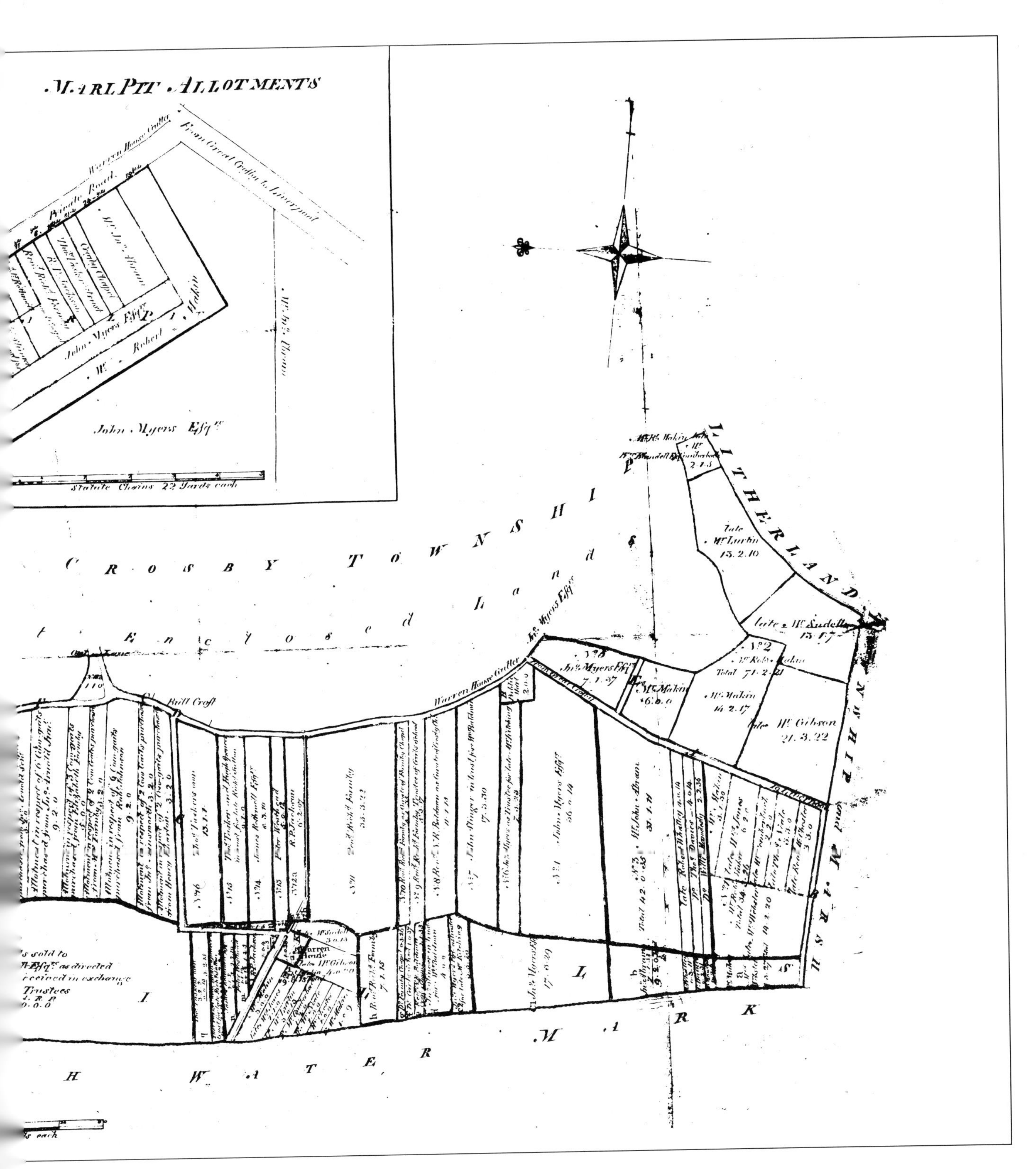

ward 1816 (AE 7/6 Lancashire Record Office)

This modest dwelling which still stands on the corner of Murat Street was the home of John Padley in 1851. Whether this is the same man as John Postlethwaite Padley from Edward Eyes' survey is not known, but it is a distinct possibility. His home was called Picton Cottage, no doubt named after Wellington's general Sir Thomas Picton who was killed at the Battle of Waterloo. In the 1851 Census, Padley is described as a house builder and may have been involved in the construction of early Waterloo.

The cottage survived, through Waterloo's development, as the home of various Victorian professionals; solicitors, gentlemen, merchants and doctors.

<u>*Sandheys*</u>

13. Sandheys (BU/SAN 1)

This was the home of a timber merchant called Richard Houghton. Born in 1809 in Liverpool, he was a partner in the firm Houghton and Smith. He built Sandheys in 1848-9 and it is described in several accounts as being part of a large estate with beautiful grounds. The entrance lodge was in Marsh Lane (now College Road), one of four lodges attached to the 14-acre estate. Indeed it was the third-highest rated building in the area, and Houghton was known locally as "Squire Houghton". The 1851 Census shows that Houghton shared his house with his wife, seven children and five servants.

The family was at the centre of a bizarre incident in Waterloo's history. On 6th May 1856, the government was testing a new howitzer on the Bootle shore. Constructed by Mr. Whitworth of Manchester, this gun could fire balls weighing between 24lbs and 48lbs. Unfortunately, the Royal Artillery officers supervising the experiment incorrectly estimated the range and pitch of the gun. Three of the balls landed in the Waterloo area. The first hit a house, the second landed next to a policeman, and the third hit a bank of earth and rebounded into Sandheys. It entered the parlour where Mrs. Houghton was sitting and caused considerable damage. Miraculously no-one was hurt in the incident.

Richard Houghton died at Sandheys in 1869, aged 58. A local story recounts that the hearse containing his coffin was wrecked by a passing train. The house that he built only survived him for another 20 years: it was demolished around 1889 and Sandheys Avenue was built over the site.

Victoria Cottage

This building still exists and is now St. Edmund's Presbytery in Oxford Road. Built around 1840 the cottage originally had an unspoilt view of the sea. It was obviously named after Queen Victoria, and the adjoining building being called Albert Cottage seems to confirm this.

Very little is actually known about Victoria Cottage except that it was the home of Lieutenant Henry G. Killack, R.N. in 1851, who lived there with his wife, six children and one servant. He was a Royal Navy officer who was born in Torpoint, Cornwall in 1788. He joined the Royal Navy in 1800 as a volunteer 3rd class aboard HMS Royal Standard, one of the ships that fought at the Battle of Trafalgar, and eventually died in Liverpool in 1858.

Seafield House

This is one building that was surprisingly, not named in the 1851 census even though it was in existence at the time, having been shown on the 1845-9 Ordnance Survey map. The 1845-9 map shows the house standing in Waterloo Park and in 1851 it was the home of Dr. John Hicks and family.

14. Waterloo Lodge (corner of Hicks Road and Crosby Road North) (RD/HICW 1)

THE MUSHROOM GROWTH OF WATERLOO

On 24th July 1848, a single track railway between Waterloo and Southport was opened by the Liverpool, Crosby and Southport Railway Company; a horse omnibus completed the connection with Liverpool. The first timetable was a modest affair, with only three trains running each way per day Monday to Saturday (10.15am first and second class only, 2.15 pm – all classes, and 5.30 pm – all classes) and two trains running on a Sunday. Local people called it the "Shrimpers Line", probably after the seaside cottage industry of shrimping that took place in the area. When the first locomotives arrived they were faced with difficult conditions in Waterloo because of the generally poor roads which were simply sandy lanes. One eye witness described how the "... heavy lorries which carried the locomotives sank up to their axles in the deep sand" (Forwood). On 1st. October 1850 the line was opened between Waterloo and Liverpool, making Waterloo more accessible to the main commercial centre. Prior to this, the journey had been by a four-horse bus which ran in the morning and evening; and in the summer, express boats also sailed along the Leeds-Liverpool canal bringing people as far as Litherland. In 1852 the single track was doubled and the service became more frequent. This in turn made the area more attractive to those people who wanted to escape the city and settle in a more rural environment. Three years later the railway was absorbed by the larger Lancashire and Yorkshire Railway Company. The site of Waterloo Station was originally alongside Brighton Road but it was moved to South Road in 1880/1 when a road bridge was constructed.

The hitherto gradual development of the area now accelerated to meet the needs of the new residents. Various public buildings such as churches, schools and hotels began to appear as the expanding population put pressure on the existing ones.

Churches

The Waterloo of the Ordnance Survey 1845-9 contained only two churches, Christ Church and the Independent Chapel. Prior to the building of these churches in 1840, the farmers, shopkeepers and lodging-house keepers of Waterloo would have made the journey to St. Thomas's Church, Seaforth (built 1815), or to the old St. Michael's Church, Great Crosby (built 1774, on the site of an earlier church), or to their own Parish Church of St. Helen at Sefton. Roman Catholic worship only took place in Waterloo from 1868. Prior to this worshippers had to travel to SS Peter and Paul (original church built 1826) in Great Crosby or to St. Benet's (from 1790's) in Netherton.

The rapid expansion of Waterloo is exemplified in the building of additional churches and chapels. The ***Wesleyan Chapel*** was opened in Wesley Street in 1857, although Wesleyan worship had been taking place earlier in a barn in the grounds of the Victoria Hotel. In 1864, two transepts were added to accommodate more worshippers. The chapel finally closed after 106 years, in 1963.

15. St. John's Church (PA 1/108)

St. John's Church was opened eight years after the Wesleyan Chapel, in 1865, on a site given by John Myers of Crosby House. Costing £3,500 to build, its licence was granted by the Archbishop of York as the usual licenser, the Bishop of Chester, had recently died. The church was enlarged in 1869, when a new transept added. In 1877 it was legally separated from the ancient Parish of Sefton, to form its own parish. The ***Congregational Church*** in Church Road arrived a year after St. John's Church although worship had been taking place in Waterloo since 1855 in a small hired chapel. The new church, which opened in 1866, seated 630 people and cost £6,500. The first Roman Catholic church came two years after that in 1868. Called the ***Chapel of St. Thomas of Canterbury*** on Great George's Road, the church building was only a temporary place of worship, built for only £900. A larger church was designed by Edmund Kirby, a Liverpool architect, and after two years' construction (at a cost of £10,000) finally opened for worship in 1877.

16. Primitive Methodist Chapel (Albert Hall), Albert Road,
(unclassified)

The ***Primitive Methodist Albert Hall*** was built in Albert Road some time before 1871 and had a chequered history. The Primitive Methodists sold the building to the "Brethren", who in turn passed the building on to the Salvation Army. However during this time the Primitive Methodist community had continued to grow and it became necessary for them to buy back the building. Meanwhile ***St. Andrew's Presbyterian Church*** was built in 1876. This church, by the Five Lamps, was demolished in 1988 when the congregation merged with that of Waterloo Baptist church.

The ***Welsh Calvinistic Methodist Church*** founded their church in 1879 in temporary premises in Dean Street, the present church on Crosby Road South being built in 1882. (Now called Bethania Welsh Presbyterian Church).

The ***Church of St. Mary the Virgin,*** Waterloo Park was originally an iron church opened in 1877. The foundation stone to a more permanent building was laid only five years later. The building was completed by W. G. Habershon in 1883 but not consecrated until 1886.

The Baptists were one of the last denominations to expand into Waterloo . They built an iron church in Oxford Road in 1891, and later erected a new **Baptist Church,** built by George Baines and Son, on Crosby Road North in 1911. The wide scope in doctrine associated with all the above churches indicates that Waterloo, by the end of the 19th century, had become a cosmopolitan place.

Houses and Hotels

The rapidly increasing population put pressure on existing housing stock and so there was an associated rise in the number of houses and hotels in the district. From sources available it is possible to plot this development.

As Baines' directory of 1825 had showed, Crosby Seabank (i.e. Waterloo), consisted of the Waterloo Hotel and a few houses in Marine Crescent, East Street, and South Road. Edward Eyes' Littoral Survey of 1826-39 listed Marine Crescent fully built, with six Waterloo cottages alongside the Royal Waterloo Hotel, five other houses in Marine Terrace, three houses at the end of Adelaide Terrace and some dwellings in the Esplanade (since demolished).

The Ordnance Survey map of 1845-49 indicated one more house (No. 13) on Marine Terrace, and a few more dwellings at the north end of Adelaide Terrace. Also marked were the Ship Victory Inn, plus the Waterloo, Bath, York and Wellington Hotels. The Liver Inn is shown in isolation, as is Picton Cottage on the un-named Wellington Street. Ten years later, Richardson's map of Waterloo showed some dramatic changes. (See fold-out map at end of book.)

It shows that all Marine Terrace (except No.'s 11 and 12) and Adelaide Terrace are complete. The Victoria Hotel has been added, but the Wellington has become the Queens Hotel.

The villas now standing on the north side of Great George's Road – Dunedin House, Wellington Villa, Rupert Villa, and Haydn Villa – had been built. Also shown are Beethoven House (where the Fire Station now stands) and Burlington House (the original building, where the office block of that name now stands).

Richardson's map also shows two houses at the south-west end of Blucher Street plus Anglesey Terrace on the still un-named Wellington Street. There are some houses on the north-east end of Mount Pleasant ("The Mount"); at the south-west end of Hyde Road, and in East Street and Bath Street. The Wesleyan Chapel has been built with three houses opposite on what became Wesley Street.

In Walmer Road, three houses on the north-west corner and one on the corner of Olive Road still stand as do six houses in South View. Richardson shows only three houses in Handfield Road, those near the north-eastern end, now numbered 51, 53 and 55. The shop fronts in Crosby Road North, opposite the modern Crosby Library, have since been added to the two houses shown on Richardson's map.

Waterloo's expansion continued and the Alexandra and Railway Hotels appear in the 1861 Census. Gore's 'Directory of Liverpool and Environs' for 1865 shows Marine Terrace completed but Beach Lawn with only three houses occupied. It is 1878 before Beach Lawn was fully built. By 1876 the Bath Hotel had become the Marine, whilst the Lion and Unicorn is merely described as *"No. 6 Church Road-T. Condliff, wine and spirits"*.

Waterloo Park

This exclusive residential area first appeared in the Liverpool directories around 1871 when the residents of 13 houses were listed. It wasn't until 1894, that the names of the houses appeared. Several well known residencies were listed.

Seafield House, one of the earliest Waterloo buildings, was then occupied by John Blackledge, a partner in the large chain of millers and bakers 'James Blackledge and Son'. The family had a strong Waterloo connection at the time. James Blackledge lived at 2 Eaton Bank, Crosby Road North, and his son James (Junior) lived at No. 3. In 1894, the company was thriving, owning a mill in West Derby and 18 bakers shops, including one in South Road.

The Convent of Notre Dame is listed under the authority of Miss Lucy Knight, Lady Superioress. The convent existed only a short while and was taken over by the Augustinian Sisters in 1902. Spetchley, the house of John Murphy, had been renamed Hatherley House by 1910. Around this time it became the Hotel Dieu Home for the Sick Poor, which was the predecessor of Waterloo Hospital.

Stonehouse was the residence of a notable local family headed by George Rollo. He was the eldest son of David Rollo, an engineer and shipbuilder.

George was born in 1853 in Glasgow and educated in Merston House, Seaforth. He married Emily Geves in 1878 and became a partner in his father's firm in 1887. In 1903 he began a long tradition of family public service by becoming a Justice of the Peace. After many years of varied public work, George Rollo died in 1935 and his mantle was taken up by his eldest daughter Florence, the only woman to be elected to Waterloo UDC and the only female mayor of the Borough of Crosby. She died in 1964, just weeks after the death of her beloved sister.

17. George Rollo (from: W. Pike "Contemporary Biographies")

The Schools

Another reflection of the rising population was the establishment of schools in the area. With more families settling in Waterloo, the need for education led to the founding of several of Waterloo's early schools. Christ Church National School, St. Thomas's School, St. John's School and the Wesleyan School all opened before 1877.

Christ Church National School

18. Christ Church National School (SCH/CHR 1)

The school in Great George's Road bears a date stone of 1842, and is featured on the 1845-9 Ordnance Survey map of the area. It was opened for working-class children of elementary age and it was divided into three departments: infants, boys and girls. In 1899 a new school building was built for the boys only, the infants and girls departments remaining at the original building.

Wesleyan School

The Wesleyan School was opened in 1866, initially with one master and 33 scholars, but this number soon expanded. It was taken over by Waterloo-with-Seaforth Urban District Council in 1923 and was finally closed in 1932. The school was demolished, the site being behind the two houses next to the Royal Hotel, where now stands a block of flats.

St. Thomas' R. C. School

19. St. Thomas's (St. Edmund's) R.C. School (SCH/STE 2)

This school in Oxford Road was built in 1872 as the parochial school of St. Thomas of Canterbury R.C. Church, and was known as St. Thomas' Mixed School. In 1906 a new infants school was opened and both schools continued to be called St. Thomas'. In 1953 a new building was opened alongside the original, which was then modernised. A year later in 1954, the school was re-named St. Edmund's Junior School.

St. John's Church of England School

This school in Wellington Street was built in 1876 at a cost of £2000. Initially, it was an infants school, but soon afterwards it became a mixed school with boys, girls and infants. In 1885 an extension was added to the existing building.

LOCAL GOVERNMENT IN WATERLOO

The area now known as Waterloo originally straddled the boundary between the ancient townships of Litherland and Great Crosby. However over the years, the community established its own identity. Local pressures resulted in the creation of a separate local government district which was carved out of Litherland in 1856 (some sources inaccurately quote this as 1863) in an early wave of local government reform. The district was governed by the Waterloo-with-Seaforth Local Board of Health, a body with limited powers. In 1874, when the boundaries were altered, an area of 54 acres was taken from Great Crosby and added to the district. Early on the board decided that the new district needed a place in which to conduct its business, and council offices were built in Great George's Road in 1861.

20. Waterloo Town Hall (PA 10/52)

The original building was re-constructed and enlarged, to become the Town Hall when, in 1894, the Board became an Urban District Council with wider powers. This council controlled the area until 1937 when Waterloo-with-Seaforth and Great Crosby combined to form the Borough of Crosby.

THE FIVE LAMPS

Now situated on the corner of Great George's Road and Crosby Road North, 'The Five Lamps' were originally placed in the middle of the road. An exact date for the creation of the lamps is unknown, but they were originally planned by Waterloo-with-Seaforth Local Board in 1859.They were probably added in the 1860s when the junction at which they stand gained prominence due to the construction of (what was to become) Waterloo Town Hall.

21. The Old Five Lamps, plus policeman and horse-trough (PA 10/150)

Why 'The Five Lamps'? This has been debated for many years. One possible explanation refers to various 'battle' road names in the area. It has been suggested that each of the five lamps originally represented a part of the Anglo-Netherlands army (British, Dutch-Belgian, Hanoverian, Brunswickers and Nassauers) that faced Napoleon at Waterloo before the arrival of Blucher's Prussians. Another theory is that the lamp standard gained its name because it stood at the intersection of five roads. The minutes of the Local Board seem to support this idea, saying *"a large lamp column be erected at the junction of the 5 roads near Mr. Bancrofts House at Seaforth"*. A plausible explanation is that the lamps obtained their name from the original design. This consisted of four lamps crossing each other, with a fifth lamp standing higher in the centre (see photograph), creating excellent lighting. The nick-name followed simply because the lighting was designed with five lamps!

In 1899, the gas lamps were replaced by electric lighting, a prestigious development of the day. In 1921 this location was chosen as the site of the war memorial; also around that time the lamps changed their appearance and were redesigned in the 'pendulous' style that today's lamps still follow.

THE NAMING OF THE ROADS

If the acquisition of the name 'Waterloo' by the area had been gradual, the naming of the streets after people engaged in the battle was even slower. While there are many references to the battle in street names and buildings, other factors have also been influential.

Topographical Names

The early names of Waterloo could be described as topographical as they refer to geographical features and prominent buildings.

Baines' 'Directory and Gazetteer of Lancaster', 1825, lists South Street, East Street, and Marine Crescent. In Title Deeds of 1827, there is reference to North Road (formerly North Street and the present Wellington Street), and South Road (formerly South Street).

22. Mount Pleasant (RD/MTP 1)

In the 1841 Census Mount Pleasant is listed, and subsequently there is a reference to the "Mount" house shown on the 1845-9 Ordnance Survey map. St. John's Church was built on the site of 'The Mount' in 1865.

The 1851 Census shows Bath Street and Bath Road, references perhaps to Bath Buildings (on the 1841 Census), the bathing machine dispute, or Greenall's original 'Bath and land' (from Eyes' Survey 1828-39). It may even have referred to the ancient but fashionable spa resort of Bath.

The early Brighton Road (and the area known as Brighton le Sands) was named after the original South coast bathing resort. This road was renamed Jubilee Road in 1935 to celebrate the silver jubilee of King George V.

Liverpool Road was the main route from Great Crosby to the city and originally extended as far south as The Liver Inn. The route from the Litherland shore northwards was Crosby Road. Around 1866 the section from Seaforth to the railway was renamed Crosby Road South; the remainder – plus the part from The Liver Inn to the junction at Merchant Taylors' School – became Crosby Road North.

Several roads obtained their names from large buildings on the site. Sandheys Avenue was named after Sandheys, the house of Richard Houghton; similarly Brooke Road was named after Brooke House, the home of Charles Horsfall.

York Road obtained its name from the York Hotel, though this had in turn been named after the Duke of York (the Grand Old Duke of York from nursery rhymes) who died in 1827.

Biographical Names

Some Waterloo streets were named after local residents who were the first settlers on the sites. From the 1851 Census, two such roads appear; Arnold's Place and Kilshaw Terrace. Arnold's Place was named after a local farming family who had obtained land in the enclosure of Crosby Marsh; the main branch of the family hailed from Moorside Farm in Great Crosby. Kilshaw Terrace commemorated John Kilshaw, a joiner by trade, who was involved in the property development in Waterloo.

Other roads named after local residents include Myers Road, after John Myers who lived at Crosby House (which now forms part of the convent and grounds of Nazareth House), and Hicks Road, after Dr. John Hicks who resided at Seafield House from around 1843.

Two later Waterloo roads were named after prominent contemporary statesmen. George Canning, who was Prime Minister and died in office after only six months in 1827, gave his name to Canning Place. Mortimer Road was renamed Curzon Road when Lord

Curzon, then Viceroy to India, visited Waterloo in 1904 and opened the Constitutional Club at the corner of South Road and 'Curzon Road'.

Gordon Road was named after Richard Houghton's wife Elizabeth Gordon.

Battle Names

Many of Waterloo's streets commemorate the famous battle of 1815 from which the area took its name.

Wellington Street and Duke Street were obviously named after the Iron Duke, Sir Arthur Wellesley, Duke of Wellington. Anglesey Terrace took its name from Wellington's general Henry William Paget, the Earl of Uxbridge and Marquis of Anglesey, who lost a leg in the battle. Picton Road (and Picton Cottage) celebrates the great British general Sir Thomas Picton who was killed at Waterloo.

Picton Cottage still stands on the corner of Murat Street which is named after one of Napoleon Bonaparte's generals. Two other generals appear in Waterloo street names. Firstly Gebhard Blucher, the Prussian general whose late arrival cut off the French right, and completed the rout of Napoleon, is remembered by Blucher Street. Secondly there are Brunswick Mews and Brunswick Parade, which may refer to the Duke of Brunswick, who fought for Wellington at the battle. It is possible that the Brunswick streets could refer to Caroline of Brunswick, George IV's unfortunate wife, although this is less likely.

One street which commemorates the battlefield itself is Hougoumont Avenue. Hougoumont was the name of the chateau which protected the right flank of the British army and was the scene of some of the heaviest fighting.

The "Royal" Names

Another group of names commemorate royal names and titles. Great George Road (later Great George's Road) recalls George III, although it has been suggested it might refer to George IV. Adelaide Terrace was begun in 1831, during the reign of William IV, and this terrace was named after his wife Adelaide. Other early arrivals on the scene were York Square, York Street and the York Hotel all named in honour of the Duke of York. Kent Street was a possible reference to Edward, Duke of Kent, the father of Queen Victoria. During the reign of Queen Victoria, Albert Road (c 1867) was named after the Prince Consort; Queen Street and Victoria Road (c1875) after the monarch herself.

A further royal connection is Alexandra Road (c1875), which was named after Princess Alexandra, the wife of Edward, Prince of Wales.

23. Adelaide Terrace (RD/AD 3)

NOTABLE BUILDINGS IN THE AREA

The Liver Hotel

The Liver Hotel is shown as the Liver Inn on the 1845-9 Ordnance Survey map, and has been a source of mystery and speculation for years. It is rumoured that it was the haunt of smugglers in the old days, but unfortunately – and not unexpectedly – there is no confirmation of this.

The first actual reference to the Liver Inn is dated 29th April 1819. John and Jane Abram, who acquired the land under the enclosure of the commons, transferred 17 acres of land and hereditaments to William Statham, in the occupation of John Worthington . Then on 11th June 1825 John Abram transferred some more land to William Statham. It was described as 12 acres of land including the dwelling house on the South-East corner of land in occupation of Daniel Waln. This is the first allusion to the building now known as The Liver Inn. The house is mentioned in various transactions but it is 1837 before there is mention of an innkeeper, Richard Westhead, and a public house ran by Francis Blundell.

In 1864 the name Margaret Dickinson appears as the innkeeper and she remains listed until 1888 when the role is taken over by Thomas R. Dickinson.

24. Crosby Road North showing the Liver Inn with, in front, a tram shelter and, to the inn's right, the single-storey old Smithy (RD/CRON 9)

The Old Smithy

The triangular piece of land formed by the eastern side of the Liver Inn and Crosby Road North was originally paved with stone setts and contained a weigh-bridge for carts. On the northern side of the triangle lay the Smithy, a long, low, single-storied building. It first appears in the 1876 Gore's 'Directory of Liverpool and Environs', listed as "John Howard, Farrier", and in the 1884 edition, rather remarkably, as "Ellen Howard, Farrier".

The Smithy had several subsequent owners. In 1906 it was occupied by J. & H. Sumner who ran a shoeing forge there; by 1913 O'Prey and Son had taken over, but they did not stay long. From 1915, Charles Wainwright and Son took over; but sometime around 1920 Wainwright closed the old smithy and relocated his business to 25 Bath Street. However, this wasn't the end of the smithy. In 1930/31 J. Roughly began a blacksmith's shop in the building called the Liver Forge; and this carried on business into the 1940's.

Park House

Park House was first listed on the 1881 Census, and it was probably quite a new building then. The first recorded owner was Richard Cornelius, a Liverpool corn merchant who, until 1880, had resided at Burlington House. Maybe Cornelius was attracted to the site by the natural pond which is still within the grounds of Park House.

In the late 1880's the house was taken over by the Sisters of Notre Dame, as a ladies school. This in turn was bought by the Augustinian Sisters in 1902 who set up a convalescent and rest home which has lasted and, indeed, expanded over the years.

Potter's Barn

This group of buildings is on the boundary between Seaforth and Waterloo, but is a notable reminder of the great battle.

The design is said to be a representation of the farmhouse, 'La Haie Sainte', on the Waterloo battlefield. It was built by William Potter in 1841.

25. Potter's Barn as a public recreation ground (PK 100)

Potter was a wealthy merchant whose firm Taylor, Potter and Co were engaged in the china trade. He lived in Everton and decided to build himself a mansion house and stables, building the stables first to accommodate his horse when he travelled to and from Liverpool. However, before the building was completed a crisis in the china trade caused his business to collapse and he was forced to discontinue the project. The land passed to Mr. Bibby who tenanted it out to a corn farmer.

On 11th July 1908 Potter's Barn was opened as a public recreation ground and has remained so to this day.

Seafield House

This was originally the home of Robert Makin, one of the founders of Waterloo (not to be confused with Seafield House, Seaforth, for many years a mental home on the foreshore). Seafield House was at the end of Makin's Lane (now Hicks Road and Back Winstanley Road). Makin was a corn merchant and entrepreneur based at 21 Brunswick Street, Liverpool. He built the house in approximately 1822, but his residence there was not long. By 1843 it had passed into the hands of Dr. Hicks, and Makin's family moved closer to their business, buying a house in Everton Village.

Dr. Hicks' family stayed at the house until about 1860, although the doctor himself was probably dead by 1851.

Waterloo Park Girl's School, subsequently Chesterfield High School Annexe, was built adjacent to the grounds of the house. The house itself was demolished on the construction of The Crescent around 1928.

Winchester House

This house (No. 13 Beach Lawn) was built in 1865 for Thomas Henry Ismay, the founder of the White Star Line, and he called it "Beach Lawn House". Ismay came to Liverpool from Maryport in Cumberland and set himself up as a ship broker. By 1860 he owned a small fleet of sailing boats and it was about this time that he first came to the area. He lived at "Enfield House", a regency type dwelling by Endbutt Lane (demolished in 1928). The family moved to "Beach Lawn House" when it was ready and remained there until 1885 when they moved to Thurstaston, Wirral, building a house there called "Dawpool". The 1881 census shows that Ismay's household consisted of his wife, three daughters, two sons, and ten servants; a sizeable household even by the standards of Victorian wealth and power. Even after this house was complete, "Beach Lawn House" remained the family's principal home because of its proximity to Liverpool. Whenever a White Star steamer passed the house she would sound her siren in salute of her owner.

26. Winchester House, no. 13 Beach Lawn (unclassified)

The Ismay coach-house still stands behind the house on the opposite side of what is now Murat Street. The origin of the building, with its striking tower, are recorded in the title deeds to Winchester House. Mr. Ismay had a grotto built of huge blocks of sandstone at the bottom of his garden. In this, fountains played in alcoves lined with mirrors, the water being supplied from a huge tank in the tower of the coach-house across the lane.

CONCLUSION

From a scattering of fishermen's cottages and small farms, Waterloo was to grow into a modest Victorian resort. In the space of a hundred years, what was once marshland became a thriving community of residents, tourists and businessmen. The development was only gradual but it was profound. Today a handful of buildings remind us of the splendour of the early town – monuments to a bygone era.

27. Carnival scene, South Road, at the turn of the century (unclassified)

APPENDIX 1

Population

The growth in the population of Waterloo is difficult to calculate accurately. The only source of early figures is the census, which began in 1801. Due to its small geographical size, Waterloo is not mentioned as an individual community, but as part of other larger areas, notably the chapelries of Great Crosby and Litherland. In later censuses, this problem is further complicated as "Waterloo" is quoted as a separate population figure, but parts of the village are still included in other districts. So while it is difficult to provide totally accurate population figures for Waterloo on its own, the data shows general trends.

Census Date	Township	Population
1801	Chapelry of Great Crosby	425
1811	Chapelry of Great Crosby	499
1821	Chapelry of Great Crosby	674
1831	Chapelry of Great Crosby	1201
1841	Waterloo	699
	Waterloo/Great Crosby	649
1851	Waterloo	859
	Waterloo/Great Crosby	816
1861	Waterloo	1317
	Waterloo/Little Brighton/ Blundellsands/ Great Crosby	1300
1871	Waterloo	2810
	Waterloo/Pt. of Brighton Le Sands	1750
1881	Waterloo-with-Seaforth	5710
1891	Waterloo-with-Seaforth	17328
1901	Waterloo-with-Seaforth	23120
1911	Waterloo-with-Seaforth	26296
1921	Waterloo-with-Seaforth	29626
1931	Waterloo-with-Seaforth	31180

APPENDIX 2

Extract from 'Spas of England' by A. B. Granville 1841

CROSBY WATERLOO

It is a village of considerable size, spread at a short distance from the low-water sands; and in front of it a long line of neat cottages, one storey high, each having a shelving verandah over the ground-floor window, presents its face to the south-western horizon.

The Waterloo Hotel, a building with somewhat more of architectural style about it than the rest, being two stories high, forms the head of or entrance into the village from the Liverpool-road. Like the other and contiguous buildings, it has between it and the beach, a large expanse of sandy soil, barely covered with short grass. Below it the sands slope gently down to the margin of the sea, and on these are seen several bathing machines arranged in a row.

The place, judging from the appearances, seems much frequented. Its aspect is westerly, inclined a little to the south. New Brighton, on the opposite, or Cheshire coast, may be plainly seen from this spot, which being situated near the embouchure of the Mersey, has constantly before it a busy and lively scene of arrivals and departures of sailing-vessels and steamers.

Behind the village the country is one universal flat, except where the eye catches, on the right, the gentle elevation on which stand some of the streets, and the more recently built houses of Liverpool. High winds blow often, and sweep along this coast, making, I should think, the marine houses somewhat uncomfortable upon the least approach of cold weather.

The principal division of the line of marine cottages before described, is called the Marine Crescent. Each cottage has a small garden in front, and then the road of communication, beyond which is the flat green already mentioned, which serves as a general promenade. An attempt was made some time since to establish a rendezvous saloon, with gentlemen's baths and billiards; but it failed, and the place in itself is probably as dull as it looks wild and deserted all round – a proper retreat, however, for quiet and sea-bathing on account of ill-health.

I examined the beds and sitting-rooms of the Waterloo, and received a card of their terms, which are very reasonable. For two pounds sixteen shillings a week, a single person may board and lodge at this house, which in every way resembles some of the best appointed hotels at other and more fashionable sea-bathing places. The coffee-room is airy and neatly appointed; the bedrooms are of moderate size, and all those on the second floor look over the sands, and are consequently preferred. Every thing in the house looks clean, including the landlady, who seems moreover a quiet and pleasing person. The means of communication with Liverpool are frequent, omnibuses come and depart every hour in the day, at the moderate fare of one shilling

APPENDIX 3

Extract from 'Romantic Tales of Old Lancashire' by Joseph Pearce (Published by the Ormskirk Advertiser in 1931)

Waterloo and Blundellsands
(ONE HUNDRED YEARS AGO)
There were twelve Crosby men sitting around our bivouac fire; it is eighteen years since that night in camp, but I remember the incident as well as if it happened but a month ago.
(A.D. 1815). Blucher had been defeated at Ligny on the sixteenth of June, but a courier brought us word that Wellington had repulsed the French at Quatre Bras.
Now the odds were even, but we knew that Napoleon would make a desperate stand at Waterloo. At the first streak of dawn we were again in the saddle and, as that most eventful day wore on, our armies met and crushed the might of France. General Picton stationed us in a wood near Hougoumont farm house, and we saw something of the gallant attack. Twice during the day Murat's men broke through our lines and were twice repulsed. As twilight came, we heard that Blucher had recovered from his temporary defeat and was hastening to the support of our "Iron Duke". Then the last effort of that day was made and I remember how the French rode across the lines of our fire as they covered the retreat of Napoleon – whose star had set.

(A.D. 1823.) As soon as we were released from service we returned to my mother's cottage on "Crosby Sea-bank" to recuperate our health. It was here that we heard that our landlord had made up his mind to give our little village the glorious name of "Waterloo" in honour of England's famous victory, all the streets are to be named after gallant generals.
'Tis said that the King himself spent a night here, and that the Earl of Derby's children enjoyed a summer holiday at the "Round House" at Blundellsands.
These are the days of winter and I must sit all day by my fireside in this ruined cottage, the French bullet in my hip keeps me in my "chimney corner" but from my little window I can see the "Marine Crescent" that they are building along the sea front of this new Waterloo.
On our table before us lies Mr. Sherriff's map dated 1823; let us see how they are laying out the land where once our cattle browsed betwixt the Rimrose brook and Blundell's beach.

(A.D. 1828) There are a few little cottages in South Road on the North side, but there is scarcely a house of any size save Warren House and Mr. Houghton's and the shed wherein lives Tim, the donkey-man, who takes charge of the bathing vans.
At the head of the "Warren House Gutter" stands Mr. Myer's house and – near by – I notice Mr. Makin's farmhouse – "Brookside" – surrounded with trees.

(A.D. 1833) The years slip by and I see the little township, called by courtesy "Brighton", rising into importance.

The building of the Royal Waterloo Hotel at the bottom of Great George's Road will make our village better known.

Folk say that the road is named after our victorious King George – I cannot see why the surveyors did not call our new street Great Wellington Street at the same time. Wellington deserves it!

John Ripley is building a cottage on Marine Terrace, so as to enjoy the sea bathing, which is becoming fashionable on this sandy beach and three of my old soldier comrades (who are blacksmiths) have built cottages in East Street, Duke Street and in York Place, so as to be near "the Mews" where the Liverpool gentry stable their nags in the summer time. There is work for three blacksmiths there.

(1841) William Potter – a native of Everton – is building a barn and coach-house on the high road – modelling his design upon the farm house which we used to call "La Haie Sainte" (the memory of that siege comes back to me, as I write of Hougoumont in Flanders).

Folk say he intended to build a mansion? Will it ever be more than "Potter's Barn", now that his wealth is reduced? So the talk wags in the "Snuggery" of the Liver Inn.

We have some promise of trade in East Street; here stand the first shops of Waterloo, the back of the property looks over the fields towards the new railway station – the terminus of the line from Southport, the railway that (folk say) will, one day, be extended to Liverpool.

(A.D. 1847.) The Scottish Presbyterians are holding services in the Assembly Rooms (The Bijou), in East Street, and I am told the Wesleyans are building a chapel in Bath Street.

As I sat one evening with my friend Wilkinson (a local historian) in the parlour of Squire Houghton's lodge by Manley's crossing, I heard the story of Squire Houghton's funeral – how the hearse containing the coffin was wrecked by a passing train.

'Twas here, also, I learnt of the accident at (old) Christ Church – one Monday morning – when a great portion of the south wall toppled over into the garden. The clinging ivy had been the cause of the mischief

(A.D. 1878.) These, then, are my memories of my village. Ere the ivy covers Queen Adelaide's Terrace, I trow that Waterloo will be a great and prosperous town – the centre of many interests. They may even build docks on Beach Lawn.

"O Earth, what changes hast thou seen!
There rolls the deep where grew the tree".

Perchance (by A.D. 1978) there may be a Sea-wall at the foot of Hall Road to protect the doomed sand-hills from the diverted Alt and from the ravages of the encroaching sea.

Glossary

Alkali, manufacture of	Alkali was used for an important number of tasks such as dyeing and producing soda ash.
Bathing machines	Basic huts on wheels in which bathers used to change into their bathing costumes. They were pulled down to the waters edge, where bathers could exit directly into the water.
Commonable pasture land	Land over which common pasture rights were held
Copyholder	Tenant who held his land by copy of court roll. These tenants were subject to the dues and rights of the Lord of the Manor.
Cow Gaits	Gates which led onto common land. In Waterloo's case, they were used to divide land on Crosby Marsh.
Crosby Marsh	Area of land situated between the coast and Crosby Road North, extended from Bibby's land in Seaforth to Blundellsands
Farrier	A blacksmith who specialised in shoeing horses.
Freeholder	A tenant who held land in 'fee-simple', free of manorial influnence
Hereditaments	Inheritance
Incumbent	The holder of an ecclesiastical benefice, usually by ordering the devotions at a particular church.
Local Board of Health	A 19th century local authority with very limited powers relating to sewerage, drainage, supply of water, burial grounds, paving, sanitary conditions, lighting, cleansing, watching, and regulating township improvement.
Messuage	A dwelling house, outbuildings, garden and in some instances land.
Primitive Methodists	A society of Methodists founded by Hugh Bourne in 1810 by secession from the main body, so called because they maintained the original methods of preaching. In 1932 they joined with the United Methodists and Wesleyan Methodists to form the Methodist Church.
Rabbit Warren	Area of land that was situated along the coast from present day Blundellsands to the River Alt. This area was infested with rabbits which were trapped for their fur and meat. The rest of the carcass was used as fertilizer.
Shrimping	A cottage industry along the coast where fishermen called 'shrimpers' specialised in catching shrimps.
Star	Now called marram grass, this plant grows well in sandy soils, flourishing on Sefton's sand dunes.
Strand	The sea shore
Warren	*see Rabbit warren*
Wesleyan	a Methodist denomination founded by John Wesley

Bibliography

Barrow, J. P. — Doctor Arthur Prime May of Crosby 1822-1884
Richard Houghton of "Sandheys", Waterloo. 1956
Seafield Hall, Seaforth. 1962
The world of John Myers, Esq of Crosby House, Great Crosby. 1948

Blair, Frederick — Some literary reminiscences of the district.

Carlyle, Jane Welsh — Letters and memorials
New selection of her letters. 1950

Census — 1841-91

Crosby Herald — Our churches: the early history and growth - St. Thomas of Canterbury. 19/5/1906, p7

Daily Post — Bibby's land and the Waterloo Council. 1904

Directory — Directory of Bootle-cum-Linacre, Crosby, Litherland, Seaforth and Waterloo. 1888

Directory — Directory of Waterloo, Blundellsands, Great Crosby and Seaforth. 1906/1909/1913

Farrar, W. — Victoria History of England: Lancashire, 1907

Fenton, S. — Seaforth: Home of the merchant princes. 1978

Forwood, W. B. — Recollections of a busy life. Reminiscences of a Liverpool shipowner. 1920

Gahan, John — Seaport to Seaside. 1985

Gollan, E. — Memories of Crosby 60 years ago.

Gore — Directory of Liverpool and environs, 1871/1869/1873/1881/1891/1895.

Granville, A. B. — Spas of England. 1841

Greatbatch, M. — The Muspratt family and the Merseyside alkali industry.

Hockenhull, N — Waterloo-with-Seaforth Local Board of Health: the beginning. 1955

Jones, M. A. — Waterloo in the borough of Crosby, Lancashire

Lamb, C. — Ancient Crosby.
The early history of Waterloo.
Story of Crosby. 1936

Lancashire & Yorkshire Railway — Specification of works requested in completing a new road at Waterloo called Brighton Road. 1882

Lawson, Janet — The history of St. John's Church Waterloo. 1965

Liverpool Archdiocese — Directory 1995

Liverpool Parish Messenger — St. Mary's, Waterloo.

McLoughlin, D. — Christ Church, Waterloo: One hundred and fifty years on.

Nightingale, B. — Lancashire Non-conformity. 1893

Oldham, W. — The Ismay Line. 1961

Pearce, Joseph — Romantic tales of old Lancashire. 1931.

Pevsner, Nikolaus — The buildings of England: South Lancashire. 1969

Pike, W. — Contemporary Biographies, 1910

Sefton MBC — Notes on Waterloo.

Stewart-Brown, R. — Pedigree of the Houghton family of Middleton and Liverpool, Co Lancs.

Tagart. E — Letter describing sea-bathing at Crosby. 1827
Letter. 1827

Tyrer, F. — Crosby Races.

Victoriae Reginae — Local government boards provisional orders confirmation act 1874.

Waterloo Methodist Circuit — A history of each church. 1936.

Waterloo-with-Seaforth Local Board of Health — Local Board of Health Provisional orders for the application of the Public Health Act to the district of Waterloo-with-Seaforth in the county of Lancashire, 1856.
Minutes 1856-92

Wilkinson, George — History of Waterloo. 1935

Urban District Council of Waterloo — Minutes 1893-1936

Index

Abram, Jane 46
Abram, John 9, 46
Adelaide Terrace 26, 37, 45, 46, 56
Albert Cottage 33
Albert Road 36,45
Alexandra Hotel 37
Alexandra Road 45
Anglesey Terrace 37, 45
Arnold Family 44
Arnold's Place 26, 28, 44
Assembly Rooms 23, 56
Augustinian Sisters 38, 48
Back Kilshaw Terrace 26
Back South Road 26
Back Winstanley Road 49
Baptist Church 36
Bath Buildings 26, 44
Bath Hotel 26, 28 37
Bathing Machines 10-13, 44
Bath Road 26, 44
Bath Street 20, 26, 37, 44, 47, 50
Beach Lawn 37, 49, 50, 56
Beach Lawn House 49
Beethoven House 37
Bethania Welsh Presbyterian Church 36
Bibby, John 20, 49
Bibby's Land 20,
Bijou Theatre 24
Bijou Electric Picture House 24
Bird, John 24
Blackledge, John 38
Blucher, *General* Gebhard 45, 55
Blucher Street 37, 45
Blundell, Francis 46
Blundell, *Colonel* Nicholas 12
Blundell, William 11, 12, 18
Brighton Le Sands 14
Brighton Road 34, 26
Brooke Road 26, 28, 29, 44
Brookside 55
Brunswick Mews 21, 22, 45
Brunswick Parade 26, 45
Burlington House 37, 48
Canning Place 44
Carlyle, Jane Welsh 12
Catterall, William 11
Census 25, 26, 28, 29, 32, 48, 53
Chesterfield High School Annexe 49
Christ Church 21, 23, 26, 35, 56
Christ Church National School 39
Church Road 36
College Road 32
Congregational Church 36
Convent Of Notre Dame 38
Copyhold 16
Cornelius, Richard 48
Cow-Gaits 7
Crescent, The 49
Crosby Borough 38
Crosby House 35, 44
Crosby Library 37
Crosby Marsh 7, 8, 16, 17, 44
Crosby Mill 16
Crosby Point 18
Crosby Road 26
Crosby Road North 26, 36, 37, 38, 42, 44, 47
Crosby Road South 36, 44
Crosby Seabank 7, 9, 13, 14, 37, 55
Crosby Seabank Company 10
Crosby Seabank Hotel see Royal Waterloo Hotel
Curzon Road 44, 45
Dawpool 49
Dean Street 36
Dickinson, Margaret 46
Dickinson, Thomas 46
Drill Hall 24
Duke Street 45, 56
Dunedin House 37
East Street 13, 23, 25, 26, 37, 43, 56
Eaton Bank 38
Emblem, James 24
Enclosure of the Commons 7, 24, 30
Endbutt Lane 49
Enfield House 49
Ennis Cottage 21, 22
Eyes, Edward 17, 18
Farriers 47
Fire Station 37
Five Lamps 36, 42
Freeholders 15, 16
Gaskell, Roger 24
Geves, Emily 38
Gladstone, John 9
Gordon Road 45
Great George's Road 11, 19, 26, 36, 37, 39, 41, 42, 45, 56
Great Wellington Street 56
Hallows, John 24
Hall Road 56
Halls the Carriers 24
Handfield Road 37
Hatherley House 38
Haydn Villa 37
Hicks, *Dr.* John 9, 44, 49
Hicks, Road 9, 34, 44, 49
Horsfall, Charles 29, 44
Hotel Dieu Home for the Sick Poor 38
Hotel Tap 26
Howard, Ellen 47
Howard, John 47
Houghton, Richard 32, 33, 44, 55, 56
Hougoumont (Belgium) 45, 55, 56
Hougoumont Avenue 45
Hyde Road 37
Jones, *Reverend* C. J. G. 21, 22
Jones, John 26
Jubilee Road 44
Independent Chapel 23, 24, 25, 35
Ismay, Thomas Henry 49
Ivy Deane 14
Kent Street 19, 45
Killack, Henry G. 33
Kilshaw, John 13, 24, 44, 18, 21, 22
Kilshaw Terrace 26, 28, 44
Knight, Lucy 38
Ladies' Guild 14
Lancashire & Yorkshire Railway Company 34
La Haie Sainte (Belgium) 48, 56
Leeds - Liverpool Canal 34
Leigh, Charles 28, 29
Litherland Marsh 21
Lion and Unicorn 37
Liver Forge 47
Liver Inn 37, 44, 46, 47, 56
Liverpool, Crosby & Southport Railway Company 34
Liverpool Road 26, 28, 44
Makin, Robert 9, 49, 55

Makin's Lane 9, 49
Manley's Crossing 56
Marine Crescent 11, 13, 15, 16, 26, 37, 43, 55
Marine Hotel 37
Marine Terrace 7, 37, 56
Marsh Lane 32
Mason Street 24
Merchant Taylors' School 44
Mersey Docks & Harbour Board 20
Mersey View 14, 26
Merston House 38
Mews, The 22, 26, 56
Moorside Farm 44
Mortimer Road 44
Mount, The 37, 44
Mount Pleasant 26, 37, 44
Murat Street 32, 45, 50
Murphy, John 38
Muspratt, James 20
Myers, John 9, 35, 44, 55
Myers Road 44
Nazareth House 44
Neal, Absolom 22, 26
Neal, Margaret 22
North Marine Terrace (see also Mersey View) 14, 26
North Road 43
North Street 43
North View 26
Olive Road 37
O'Prey & Son 47
Oxford Road 33, 40
Padley, John 19, 32
Park House 48
Picton Cottage 26, 28, 29, 32, 37, 45
Picton Road 45
Picton, *Sir* Thomas 32, 45
Potter, William 20, 48, 56
Potter's Barn 20, 48, 49, 56
Primitive Methodist Chapel 23, 36
Queen's Hotel see Wellington Hotel
Queen Street 45
Rabbit Warren 7, 17
Railway Hotel 37
Registry of Domestic Service 14
Rimrose Brook 18, 55
Ripley, John 56
Rollo, David 38
Rollo, Florence 38
Rollo, George 38
Rothwell, *Reverend* Richard 7, 12
Roughley, J. 47
Round House 55
Royal Hotel see Royal Waterloo Hotel
Royal Seaforth Docks 20
Royal Waterloo Hotel 9, 10, 11, 13, 19, 26, 28, 37, 39, 54, 56
Rupert Villa 37
Salvation Army 24
Sandheys 26, 28, 32, 33, 44
Sandheys Avenue 33
Scottish Presbyterians 56
Seafield House 9, 33, 38, 44, 49
Seaforth Hall 20
Seaforth House 9
Sefton, *Earl of* 11, 17
Ship Victory Inn 21, 22, 26, 37
Shrimping 34
Shrimpers Line 34
Sisters of Notre Dame 48
Smithy 47
South Road 19, 26, 28, 34, 38, 43
South Street 13, 37, 43
South View 37
Southwell Cottage 21
Spetchley 38
St. Andrew's Presbyterian Church 36
St. Benet's Church, Netherton 35
St. Edmund's R. C. Junior School 40
St. Edmund's R.C. Presbytery 33
St. John's Church 35, 36, 44
St. John's School 39, 40
St. John's Sunday School 23
St. Helen's Church, Sefton 35
St. Mary the Virgin Church 36
St. Michael's Church, Great Crosby 35
SS Peter and Paul R.C. Church, Great Crosby 35
St. Thomas's Church, Seaforth 35
St. Thomas of Canterbury R.C. Chapel 36
St. Thomas of Canterbury R.C. Church 40
St. Thomas's R.C. School 39, 40
Statham, William 46
Stonehouse 38
Sumner, J. & H. 47
Taylor, Potter and Co. 49
Victoria Cottage 26, 28, 33
Victoria Hotel 35, 37
Victoria Road 45
Volunteer Canteen 23, 24, 25
Waddington, Richard 23, 24
Wainwright, Charles 47
Walmer Road 37
Waln, Daniel 46
War Memorial 43
Warren Gutter 16, 17
Warren House 11, 55
Warren House Gutter 55
Waterloo Amateur Dramatic Society 23
Waterloo Baptist Church 36
Waterloo Hospital 38
Waterloo Hotel see Royal Waterloo Hotel
Waterloo Lodge 34
Waterloo Park 36, 38
Waterloo Park Girl's School 49
Waterloo Road 21
Waterloo Station 34
Waterloo Terrace 26
Waterloo Town Hall 41, 42
Waterloo-with-Seaforth Local Board of Health 12, 41, 42
Waterloo-with-Seaforth Urban District Council 12, 14, 20, 38, 39, 41
Wellington, *Duke of* 9, 32, 45, 55
Wellington Hotel 26, 37
Wellington Street 37, 40, 43, 45
Wellington Villa 37
Welsh Calvanistic Methodist Church 36
Wesleyan Chapel 35, 37, 56
Wesleyan School 39
Wesley Street 35, 37
Westhead, Richard 11, 46
White Star Line 49
Winchester House 49, 50
Worthington, John 46
York Hotel 26, 37, 44, 45
York Place 56
York Road 44
York Square 28, 45
York Street 28, 45

28. Map: W. A. Richardson: Waterloo Local Board of Health District 1857 (M 313)